You cannot see God, but get to know Jesus - He is the exact image of God!

ISBN: 979-8-9922853-8-3 - Paperback
ISBN: 979-8-9922853-9-0 - Hardcover

NBeirene Press

Jesus!

By Nancy Owusu Adu

Illustrated by Christina Rudenko

Jesus is The Door

The door that brings salvation.
Through Jesus I can enter
into the good life God has for me.

I am the door, if anyone enters in by me, he will be saved.
John 10:9a WEB

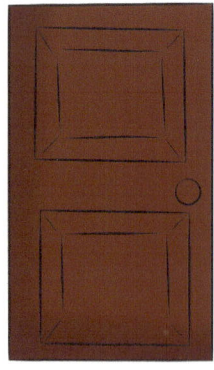

Jesus is a Strong Tower

A tower to lean on for safety.
A tower to run to in times of need.

The Lord's name is a strong tower,
when I run to it, I am safe.
Proverbs 18:10

Jesus is The Way

The way that leads to eternal life.
I will follow everywhere He leads

Jesus said to him, "I am the way, the truth, and the life.
No one comes to the Father, except through me.
John 14:6 WEB

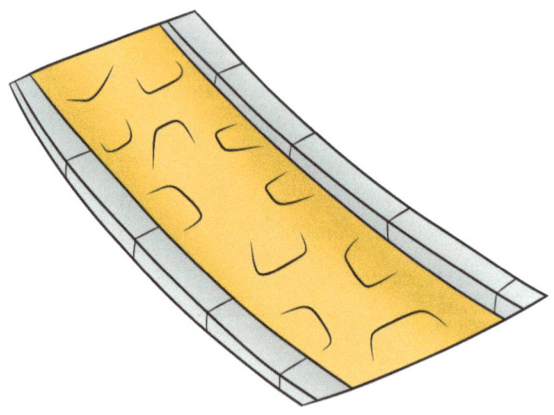

Jesus is The Bread of Life

Bread that satisfies.
Jesus fills me with blessings everyday!

Jesus said to them, "I am the bread of life.
Whoever comes to me will not be hungry,
and whoever believes in me will never be thirsty.

John 6:35 WEB

Jesus is a Shield

A shield to cover and protect.
With Jesus as my shield, nothing can harm me!

God's way is perfect and pure,
He is a shield to all who trust Him.
Psalm 18:30

Jesus is The Word

The Word that created everything
The Word that gives life to all.

**The word became a human being and lived among us,
and we saw His Glory!**
John 1:14a

Jesus is The True Vine

A vine to nourish me.
Staying connected to Jesus keeps me growing!

I am the vine. You are the branches.
He who remains in me and I in him bears much fruit.
John 15:5 WEB

Jesus is The Gate

The Gate that keeps out all the bad stuff.
A gate to keep me secure.

I am the gate; anyone who enters through me will be safe.
John 10:9

Jesus is The Rock

The rock that keeps me safe.
Doing what He tells me to do is like
building my life on a rock!

He is the rock and perfect in all His ways.
Deuteronomy 32:4

Jesus is The Light

A light to shine in darkness.
A light to give direction.

"I am the light of the world.
He who follows me will not walk in the darkness
but will have the light of life."
John 8:12 WEB

Jesus is
The Chief Cornerstone

He is so important to me
And holds every part of my life together.

Jesus Christ is the chief corner stone.
Ephesians 2:20

Jesus is The Son of God

He is the only way to the Father
and more than enough for me!

For God so loved the world that He gave His only Son,
that anyone who believes in Him should not die but live forever!
John 3:16

About the Author

"This will be written for the generation to come, that a people yet to be created may praise the Lord"
Psalm 102:18 NKJV

Nancy Owusu Adu is a Christian writer, a wife and mother of 3.
With over 2 decades of experience teaching Sunday school,
Nancy is passionate about bringing God's Word to life for both the young
and young at heart. Among her published Children's books are titles such as
God's Word Is, Jesus Gives Me, Who is Jesus to me, and many more.
Outside of writing, Nancy enjoys reading, traveling,
and connecting with family and friends.

Follow Nancy to stay connected
Instagram @ nancy.owusuak
Facebook @ Nancy Owusu Adu

www.ingramcontent.com/pod-product-compliance
Lightning Source LLC
Chambersburg PA
CBHW041608120626
46551CB00002B/352